How to SUP With Your PUP

by Maria Christina Schultz

Published by Maria Christina Schultz
Fredericksburg, Va., USA

www.SUPwithPUP.com

ISBN: 978-0615787718

Cover design and book design by Maria Christina Schultz

Photographs by John and Maria Schultz unless otherwise credited. All photographs are copyrighted and cannot be used or reproduced without written permission from the author or credited photographer.

Disclaimers

The purpose of this book is to help people safely enjoy the sport of stand up paddling with their dogs. With guidance from veterinarians, dog trainers, and paddling instructors, this book aims to give a general understanding of the sport and what is involved when paddling with a dog. This book cannot cover every possible element about stand up paddling or dog training. The author is not a veterinarian and is not qualified to offer medical advice. Suggestions made in this book should not replace professional veterinary care. While every effort has been made to create a solid training plan, each dog is different and will respond differently to training. The author and publisher are not liable for any adverse effects or injuries you or your dog may experience from the information contained in this book. Outdoor activities can be risky and should be entered into with caution.

Dogs have been referred to as male dogs in this book for consistency and to relate to Riley's story. Female dogs are just as awesome and can learn to paddle just as well as male dogs. We didn't forget about the female dogs out there!

Brands have not been named in this book but are present in many of the photographs. These are not necessarily endorsements. Readers should purchase gear that suits their own comfort, needs, and budget.

To Riley, my best friend.
And to all the incredible dog guardians who
never leave their best friends at home.
See you on the water!

Table of Contents

For the last six years, Riley and I have been unstoppable: We hike, bike, swim, run, do agility, read to children at the library. The list goes on and on. There's little we don't do as a team, and even less that Riley can't do. He's fast and smart and willing to try anything. While rock climbing with Riley, I'd look up over the top of a boulder to see him waiting for me to finish, as if to say, "You know there's an easier way up the back, right?" After each adventure, we'd race each other back to the car, share the last bit of water and granola in my pack, and head home tired and a little bit closer to each another.

Last summer I needed a new outdoor hobby. It had to give me a good workout, and I wanted to have Riley along. Stand up paddleboarding! I loved the idea of being on the river, and that Riley might be into it as well (since I think he's part fish). After hours of research, I chose an inflatable board for us. A week before Memorial Day the box arrived; I unrolled the board in the living room, inflated it, and went right to work introducing Riley to the new gear.

All week we sat on the board, stood on the board, jumped on the board, jumped off the board, and did everything I could think of to make sure Riley thought that board was the coolest thing ever. That weekend we headed to the Shenandoah River. I was nervous: I had never tried this before. What if Riley had a bad experience? What if he hated it? Riley wiggled and howled as I put the board in the water and tried it. What a sensation! I was walking on water! The glide, the closeness to nature, the quiet sound of my paddle pulling through the water. It was magical. Now came the true test: Would Riley like this? Could we stay balanced on the board together? I called Riley. He jumped right on just like we had practiced in the living room, but the board moved! He did a whole Bambi-on-ice maneuver and immediately fell off. "Oh boy," I thought, "Let's try again." I sat on the board and pulled out a handful of treats. Riley hesitated, but with some coaxing he got back on! We sat on the board and floated until he seemed relaxed enough for me to kneel, then stand. The rest is history—from that first time I stood up and paddled us down river, he was so relaxed, so calm, it was clear he was having the same feeling I was. And like me, he was completely taken by this new sport.

photo by Shawn Young

After Memorial Day, we were on the river every weekend. I paddled down river; he jumped off and swam, then ran along the banks to catch up with me. It was a perfect summer! By the end of the season, our beloved inflatable board was leaking, and I noticed Riley was slowing down a little. Oh, well, I wanted a faster, newer board anyway. I wanted to push myself and paddle farther and faster. So I decided to upgrade to a sleek and narrow race board—something not dog friendly—but I would buy a new board for Riley next summer.

About a week after receiving the new board in the early fall, Riley had his annual checkup. I told the vet he seemed less eager to run by the end of the summer, and something seemed off. After his exam and some X-rays, we got news that swallowed the air in the room and filled my eyes with water—Riley has hip dysplasia. Wait. What? No! How can that be? He's so athletic nothing stops him from doing anything.

I felt awful; his slowing down was a result of arthritis that was developing in his hips. The best thing we could do for him, the vet said, was to keep his legs strong and muscular. And one of the best activities would be swimming. Suddenly paddling without Riley didn't seem fair or much fun at all. I had to trade the new board in and get something we could paddle on through the fall so Riley could keep swimming. I told this story to the retailer I purchased the board from, and through some wonderful customer service, they let me exchange the race board for a fast and stable dog-friendly one. Good thing outdoor retailers tend to be dog lovers, too!

Now Riley takes an anti-inflammatory medication, and we supplement with wild salmon oil to manage his arthritis. He's doing remarkably better, and we've been paddling and swimming year round. Riley still has miles of adventure ahead, but we just might need to slow down a little. I realized it's not how far or how fast you go, it's the company you keep that makes the adventure special. I wouldn't trade a day on a super-fast board for a slower day with my best friend. Seeing Riley dance in circles and howl when I put the board on the car is all I need.

Over the last several years, stand up paddling (SUP) has become the fastest-growing water sport in the world. Originating in Hawaii, SUP has reemerged from the 1960s because of its simplicity to learn. Everyone from serious athletes to children is learning to SUP—even the family dog! People are enjoying the sport because it offers a total body workout combined with the peacefulness of being on the water. Stand up paddling is unique because it can be relaxing and low-key or as rigorous and challenging as you want it to be. It's a sport that offers something for everyone. Even if you aren't athletic, the learning curve is fast, and most dogs pick it up pretty quickly, too. However, learning to balance together is a little more involved, and that's what this book is for.

Paddling with your dog is a great way to bond. While out on the water, it's just you, the board, and your dog—who will love the individual attention. For Riley and me, it also offers a chance for some extra swimming, which is great exercise for dogs with arthritis and older dogs with joint pain. Dogs young or old, large or small can enjoy riding with you on the water. There are just a few things you'll want to keep in mind before getting started.

• **Check with your veterinarian.** Make sure your dog is in good shape. Like us, they will be using their core muscles and leg muscles to balance on the board. Their legs will get a workout from jumping on and off the board along with any swimming they do. Check to be sure your dog is properly vaccinated and that he's current on monthly preventives for heartworms, fleas, and ticks. Enjoying the outdoors and the water with your dog also means being exposed to bacteria and other bugs. Regular fecal examinations are important to check for intestinal parasites.

 "A good pup is a tired pup! Our loyal companions need to be stimulated mentally as well as physically. These turn out to be the best and most stable family pets."
— Helen Jewett, DVM, Hartwood Animal Hospital

- **Be certain that your dog is comfortable in the water and can swim.** Chances are, at some point, you will both fall in. If your dog doesn't like the water or getting wet, you will first need to work on desensitizing your dog to water. This book does not cover how to teach your dog to swim or how to desensitize dogs to water. If your dog needs help getting comfortable around the water, seek assistance from a certified trainer.

- **Do some basic training.** Training is more likely to succeed if your dog can reliably obey the sit-stay, down-stay, and on and off commands. Your dog may be sitting on the board with you for long periods of time. Making sure he's content until you release him will make paddling more enjoyable for both of you.

- **Purchase the right gear.** Select a board that will be stable for you and your dog. A long, wide board is probably your best bet. Having the right gear will help your dog feel comfortable and confident on the board. The next section takes a closer look at boards and gear that work best for dogs.

- **Make sure your dog is comfortable in a life jacket.** Your dog should always wear a life jacket or personal flotation device (PFD) when paddling. If your dog has never worn one before, think about introducing it ahead of time.

- **Practice some off-leash manners.** When your dog is on the board, you won't want him on a leash. If your dog were to fall overboard, the leash could get caught on something and hold him underwater or choke him. Many states have leash laws, so you may need to have your dog on a leash until you are in the water. Your dog's good off-leash manners can help avoid any trouble.

 TIP – If your dog has never worn a life jacket, gradually introduce him to it. Only put it on for short periods of time, then slowly increase the time. Play with your dog while he has it on, and reward him.

Purchasing the right gear is important to the success of paddling with your dog. Your dog will feel more confident if he's comfortable, and you'll have an easier time paddling with the right equipment.

PFD (for you) - The U.S. Coast Guard considers stand up paddleboards vessels. Therefore, you are required to carry a PFD, whistle, and distress light on board when you are outside surf, swim, and bathing zones. Always wearing a PFD is good practice anyway, especially when your dog is on board. If your dog makes an unexpected movement, you can easily be thrown off balance and fall off your board. Traditional jacket-style PFDs are fine but can become bulky and warm on long paddles. Smaller inflatable belt pack PFDs are a great option and are becoming increasingly popular with stand up paddlers. Many belt pack PFDs have pockets, allowing you to store your whistle, lights, and dog treats.

Not only do PFDs help your dog swim, they also make your dog more visible. If your dog gets separated from you when out paddling, a brightly colored jacket can help you and boaters spot him.

PFD (for your dog) - Since you are required to carry a PFD, it's only fair your dog gets one, too. There are many great brands to choose from, but make sure your dog's PFD has a big, strong handle on the top of the jacket. This will become invaluable as you help your dog on and off the board and position him once on the board. A leash attachment point and a light loop are also nice features to look for. Be sure the jacket has a good snug fit, not too tight and not too loose.

Board Leash - Many states and parks require board leashes if you are in ocean surf. Like the PFD, the board leash is important for safety. It will keep you and your board together if you fall off. There are two different types of board leashes, straight and coiled. Straight leashes are most appropriate for use in ocean surf zones. You won't want to use a straight leash in flatwater for a number of good reasons. First, they can get wrapped around your paddle, tree stumps, or objects in the water, creating a dangerous situation for you and your dog. Straight leashes can also create drag if they hang off your board. In flatwater, coiled leashes are a safer option because they are shorter and don't hang off your board. Do not wear leashes when paddling in whitewater, and never attach the leash to your calf or ankle in moving water. In moving water, attach the leash to your waist or your PFD with a quick release harness. **A note about whitewater:** *I strongly recommend that you and your dog do not attempt to paddle together in whitewater. Rocks, shallow water, and fast-moving water are very dangerous. Do not attempt whitewater paddling until you've had specialized training first.*

Water - You and your dog will both need lots of water while paddling in the hot sun. Sun reflecting off the water can dehydrate you both quickly. Hydration packs are great options; you can easily access your water, plus it stays a little cooler inside the pack. Also be sure to get a collapsible water bowl for your dog. This makes it easier for your dog to drink, and it's lightweight to carry. Traditional water bottles work fine on shorter outings, and you can clip a bottle to your board if you have tie-downs.

Sunblock - Believe it or not, dogs can get sunburned. Put sunblock on your dog in areas where his fur is thinner—like ears and noses. Remember to reapply if you will be out in the sun for an extended amount of time. Dogs with thin hair, no fur, or pink skin are more prone to sunburn. Check with your veterinarian for sunblock brands and the amount to use on your dog.

First Aid Kit - Have a small first aid kit if you are going out on a long day trip. Anything from snakebites to torn pads can happen while your dog is out with you. Having a few supplies on hand can make all the difference until you can get back to your car. See page 27 for a list of supplies.

Dry Bag - Whatever you bring along is almost guaranteed to get wet. Things like cameras and cell phones will stay dry when strapped down in a dry bag.

Additional Items - If you are paddling at night, you are required by the U.S. Coast Guard to have a navigation light if outside surf, swim, or bathing zones. Waterproof cameras are fun to take along on paddling trips—you'll be amazed at how much wildlife you'll see.

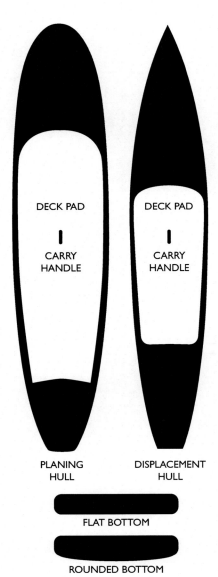

DECK PAD

CARRY
HANDLE

DECK PAD

CARRY
HANDLE

PLANING
HULL

DISPLACEMENT
HULL

FLAT BOTTOM

ROUNDED BOTTOM

Choosing the right board for you and your dog

There are many different styles of boards to choose from depending on the types of conditions you will be paddling in and the size of your dog.

The three main categories of boards are displacement hulls, planing hulls, and inflatables. Displacement hulls work best on flatwater and look more like thin kayaks or sailboats. Planing hulls look more like surfboards and handle surf and choppy water better than displacement hulls. Inflatables are just what they sound like: rubber boards that roll out and are inflated with a pump. The the rubber surfaces of inflatable boards offer better traction for paws, and they are tough enough to resist scratches from dogs' nails.

Any style of board will work with small dogs, but here are some tips to keep in mind for bigger dogs. The longer and wider the board, the more stable it will be, making it easier to balance with a dog. While a long and narrow board will offer more glide, it will be harder to balance with a big dog. Narrow boards are more tippy and usually designed for racing or more advanced paddlers. If you are going to paddle with a bigger dog, your best bet is to find something that's long (between 11 and 12.5 feet) and fairly wide. Here's an example: I weigh108 pounds, and Riley is pretty big at 52 pounds. We paddle on an 11.5-foot board that's 32-inches wide. Our board is considered wide by most standards, but I find it to be a comfortable width to keep the board stable when Riley moves.

Another design element of paddleboards that affects stability is the shape of the bottom. Many displacement hulls have rounded bottoms, making them faster in the water but harder to balance. If you are going to purchase a board for you and your dog, look for a board with a flat bottom—it will be a more stable choice.

Weight is also a factor to consider. Many boards have suggested weight capacities, so calculate your weight plus your dog's weight to make sure the total is within the board's limits. Our board is rated for 230 pounds, and our combined weight is 160 pounds. Since we are well within the weight limit, the board doesn't displace a lot of water, keeping it easy to paddle.

Deck pads are important to consider when purchasing a board for your dog to ride on. Some boards have full deck pads; these are great because they keep your dog from slipping on the traditional polished tops. Soft tops, where the entire deck is covered in a soft foam, are also a great option. However, most deck pads only cover about two-thirds to three-quarters of the board. The unpadded parts of the board will most likely have a polished finish that's slippery for paws. If your dog is anything like mine, at some point he'll venture up to the nose or move around. I recommend purchasing additional traction pads for the uncovered areas of the board. These can be purchased at any surf shop or online surf retailer. A cheaper alternative could be a rubber bath mat, a wet towel, or rubber flooring.

Here's our 11.5-foot board. We added an extra traction pad on the nose and deck rigging to hold extra gear on longer paddles.

Tie-down points are a fantastic little option that a lot of boards come with. Threading a bungee cord through the tie-down points offers a secure way to hold extra gear, like a first aid kit, extra water, and a camera. When shopping for a board, this is a feature worth considering.

 TIP – If you have a large, furry dog who enjoys swimming, like Riley, he'll be a lot heavier when he's wet. Factor in an extra 5-10 pounds for a wet dog.

Here's a summary of each type of board and its pros and cons:

Displacement Hulls: Usually designed for racing and touring, displacement hulls tend to be narrow, making them more of a challenge to balance. Generally, displacement hulls are for more advanced paddlers. If you are an advanced paddler and have a small dog, this may be the board for you.

Pros: Most efficient to paddle in flatwater, and best for long trips.
Cons: Generally less stable, especially if they have a rounded bottoms.
    Larger and thicker, making them more difficult to carry and load onto vehicles.

Planing Hulls: Designed more like traditional surfboards, planing hulls are great for anyone wanting to paddle surf. Still great in flatwater, they just won't be as fast as displacement hulls. A long and wide planing hull is the best option for novice paddlers. If you are a novice and have a large dog, you may want to start looking here.

Pros: Most stable option for paddling with a large dog.
    If you plan on sharing your board, this type is great for all ages and abilities.
Cons: Can be heavy.

Inflatables: Come in a variety of shapes and sizes, but most tend to be a planing hull design. If you don't want the hassle of loading a board on and off a vehicle, this is a great option. Inflating the board can be a bit of work, so plan for extra time to inflate your board before each paddle.

Pros: Great for traveling, easy to take anywhere.
    Durable. You won't worry about dings and scratches.
    The rubber surface is great for dogs, with less slipping.
    Good for rivers or paddling in shallow water, where you may run into rocks.
Cons: Not as efficient to paddle as displacement hulls and planing hulls.
    Over time they can develop leaks, but most come with repair kits.

Riley and I practiced for an entire week in our living room. By the weekend, he looked confident and excited on the board.

Starting on land

The idea of training with your dog on land is to gradually get him comfortable and confident on the board through positive reinforcement. The more good experiences your dog has on the board before you hit the water, the more confident he'll be when it becomes more challenging. Move slowly through the training steps; moving too fast could result in injury or negative experiences and set your training back. If your dog has never worn a life jacket, the first week is a great opportunity to get him used to wearing one. Some dogs may already be confident and not require as much work as others, but it's always wise to have a solid foundation of basic skills first.

Associating the board with fun things will help teach your dog to love it.

After you purchase your board, your first task is to get your dog on it without any coaxing. To start, bring the board into his favorite part of the house or into the backyard. Make sure it's a place that your dog enjoys being in. Lay the board flat on the ground (without the fin) and let your dog check it out. Don't force him to get on the board right away. Just let him explore it on his own. After some time has passed, place some treats or his favorite toys on the board. Let your dog take the treats or toys off of it. When he decides to walk on the board, reward him! This is what you want to see: your dog willingly getting on the board. This step could take anywhere from a few minutes to several hours. Some dogs are more cautious than others; if your dog is unsure, be patient and stay positive. Keep these sessions short or your dog may get overwhelmed, especially if he is timid. Keep your dog excited with toys and treats. You can make a trail of treats leading to the center of the board with a jackpot of cookies at the end, feed your dog meals on the board, or put a favorite pillow or dog bed on it.

You'll need to have a command that tells your dog when it's safe to get on the board and a separate command telling him when to get off. We use "hop on" and "hop off." These commands are very important for the water. If your dog unexpectedly jumps on or off the board, it could cause you to lose balance and fall off. When your dog jumps off, his back legs really kick the board back. I've fallen off plenty of times from Riley jumping before I was ready. Work this into your training from the start by always giving the "hop on" command as your dog is getting on the board, and your "hop off" command as he is getting off.

When your dog gets on the board on cue without any hesitation, start having him sit-stay and down-stay on the board. Ideally, you will want to get your dog used to being on the center of the board, which is near the handle. Start by asking your dog to get on the board, to sit, and stay, and then reward him after just a few seconds. Don't let him off the board until you give your "hop off" command. Practice this series of steps, alternating between sit-stays and down-stays. Over the course of the week, gradually increase the time you ask your dog to stay on the board.

Once you see that your dog is comfortable on the board in the house, probably after about three days, move the board to a different location inside or outside. Having training sessions in different areas will teach your dog that the lessons apply in many places; this will help transfer the cues and commands to the water.

By about the third or fourth day, your dog should be pretty comfortable getting on the board and sitting or lying on it for 15 to 20 seconds. Another element to introduce on about Day 4 is to raise the board up off the floor, so your dog gets used to jumping upward onto it. Place couch cushions under the board to raise it, or put the board up on a bed.

Practice in multiple locations. This will help your dog understand how to apply these skills in new environments.

Around Day 5, try putting it all together on land. Include your dog's PFD and the paddle so that your dog understands that the gear goes together.

Around Day 5, you'll want to add one more very important element to the training—you! The last step before heading to the water is to get on the board with your dog on land. Use your command to tell the dog it's OK to get on the board. Have him sit-stay, then stand on the center of the board behind your dog. Pet your dog and reward him. Try this a few times and make sure your dog is comfortable having you right behind him. Alternate whether you or your dog hops on the board first, then alternate who hops off the board first. Again, you'll want to increase the time you stand on the board with your dog during each session. Once your dog is relaxed with you on the board, try moving around. Move from side to side, jump up and down—shake things up. It's not always going to be smooth paddling, so the more you prepare your dog on land, the more prepared you'll both be in the water. You can even practice your stroke with a paddle so your dog becomes comfortable with the paddle passing over his head. Remember to keep rewarding your dog for all new scenarios. This helps your dog know he's doing the right thing and keeps him engaged.

After about a week, if your dog willingly gets on the board, stays in position until you release him, and is comfortable with you on the board and moving around, then you're ready to head to the water!

Here's a sample schedule for your first week training on land:

Practice the following steps two or three times a day. Keep it short. You don't need to go over 10 minutes per session. If your dog gets upset or stressed at any point, stop the session, but end on a good note. Always be positive in training. You want your dog to think the board is the coolest thing ever—which, of course, it is!

Day 1 - Get familiar with the board. Bring the board into your living room or backyard and let your dog inspect it. Place treats and toys on the board and reward your dog if he gets on the board on his own.

Day 2 - Introduce your "hop on" and "hop off" commands. Decide what commands you will use and practice using those commands as your dog gets on and off the board. Be consistent and always use the same command each time.

Day 3 - Get on and off the board on cue with short sit-stays and down-stays in between. Keep using your "hop on" and "hop off" commands, but ask your dog to sit-stay or down-stay for several seconds each time. Consider raising the board off the floor between Days 3 and 4.

Day 4 - Get on and off the board on command with longer sit-stays and down-stays in between. Repeat everything you did on Day 3, except lengthen the time you ask your dog to stay on the board. Try working up to 15 to 20 seconds. Also start training in different areas of the house.

Day 5 - Stand on the board with your dog. Alternate who gets on first and who gets off first. Continue using your "hop on" and "hop off" commands with long sit-stays and down-stays. Try working up to more than 30 seconds.

Day 6 - Get comfortable with some added movement. Continue with the objectives from Day 5, but start adding some movement on the board and introduce the paddle. Keep alternating your routine to keep it interesting and challenging for your dog.

Day 7 - Reinforce what you've learned. By this day your dog should be very comfortable on the board. Repeat everything from the past 6 days and continue rewarding your dog.

To maximize the chances of a successful first outing, pick a quiet lake or river with few distractions and little current.

Moving to the water

Now that your dog is comfortable wearing a a life jacket, staying on the board, and being on the board with you, it's time to head to the water. I strongly recommend taking your stand up paddle board out several times by yourself before bringing your dog, especially if you have never paddled before. This gives you a chance to establish some muscle memory and get comfortable with your own balance.

For the first water outing with your dog, choose a shallow, quiet river or lake on a day with low winds. Lake beaches or boat ramps are great places to start. If the ocean is your only choice, go early in the morning while the surf is small and before crowds build up. Stay away from reefs or any large rocks in the shallow water. Before you put the board in the water, set it on the beach or grass and run through the routine you practiced in your living room. Do this a few times to make sure your dog is still comfortable on the board in a new environment. If your dog is unsure or a little stressed, don't put him in the water until he's ready. You don't want your dog's first experience in the water to be a bad one.

Riley was surprised that the board moved the first time he hopped on it in the water. This was the hardest step for him. It was also the hardest step for Kona, pictured above. If your dog is having trouble with this step, place the board in very shallow water in the sand so it moves even less, and stay in shallow water until your dog feels comfortable.

Next, put the board in shallow water and stand next to it, holding it steady as you call your dog over and give your command to "hop on" the board. When your dog jumps on the board for the first time, it's going to feel different for him. The board is going to move, so be sure to praise your dog and treat him. Continue to praise him as long as he stays on the board. If your dog stays on the board for more than a few seconds, slowly push him around so he gets a feel for the movement, then give the command to release him. After your dog gets off the board, throw a party! Get really excited, because he's just made it through the hardest part. That first time getting on the board in the water can be scary, so be sure to let him know how awesome he is!

The last step is for you and your dog to get on the board together. Get on the board first and sit slightly behind the center or handle. Give your dog the "hop on" command and position him in a sit-stay right in front of you. Stay seated and paddle the board around like a kayak for a while, remembering to praise and treat the entire time. Sitting lowers your center of gravity and makes the board less tippy for your dog's first ride with you. Paddle in the seated position until you and your dog are comfortable.

A good middle step before standing is kneeling. Go from the seated position into a kneel by placing the paddle lengthwise on the board and leaning forward to place your feet underneath you. Remember to move slowly as you change positions. Stay kneeling until you both feel comfortable before trying to stand. To stand up, do the same thing you did to kneel: Place the paddle lengthwise on the board, place your hands in front of you, bring your feet in toward your hands, and slowly stand up. You will want to have your feet placed about shoulder width apart, a few inches from the sides of the board. Keep your knees slightly bent to help maintain your balance.

Standing up on the board is by far the most challenging position with your dog. If either you or your dog is unsure, don't move on until you are ready. Going from the sitting position to standing could take a few days— and that's perfectly OK. Rushing the process may mean more falls in the water, and it could stress you both out. Take your time—your dog will let you know when he's ready.

Only move from one position to the next after you both feel ready.

Here's a summary for training in the water:

The most important thing to keep in mind when you get to the water is to take these steps as slowly as you need to. There's no suggested length of time for each of these steps, so don't move on until you and your dog are ready.

Step 1 - Choose a quiet lake or river with a shallow area for your first water outing. Select a spot with minimal distractions.

Step 2 - Take the board to a safe area near the water and practice getting on and off the board on command, along with sit-stays and down-stays. Remember to reward and praise your dog.

Step 3 - Put the board in shallow water. Holding it steady, give your dog the "hop on" command. As long as your dog stays on the board, push him around in the shallow water for a while.

Step 4 - Sit on the center of the board without your dog, then give the "hop on" command. Have your dog sit in front of you and paddle for a while in the seated position.

Step 5 - Go from the seated position to a kneel, and paddle around for a while. Be certain your dog is relaxed before you try to stand.

Step 6 - Move from a kneel to a stand, staying on the center of the board. Stay in a shallow area if possible until you both feel comfortable with each other.

Step 7 - Celebrate!

"One of the best ways to bond with your dog is through play. Activities like paddling allow both the human and the dog to experience something new together. Training such as this also builds trust—another key ingredient to bonding."
— *Marlene Brock, dog trainer and handler*

Positioning your dog on the board

The weight of your dog will determine the best place for him to ride. If your dog is small, less than 20 pounds, it really doesn't matter where he prefers to sit. A larger dog will make paddling harder depending on where he positions himself. The best place for a big dog to ride is on the center of the board right in front of you. This keeps the weight on the board centered, which makes tracking, or going straight, a lot easier. Many dogs, including mine, like to ride up on the nose of the board. This is fine, but a big dog will cause the nose to sink into the water, making it more difficult to track. The most important idea, though, is to encourage your dog to stay centered, whether on the nose or right under you. If your dog sits too far right or too far left, it will make your job of balancing and paddling straight more difficult. Dogs that ride on the back of the board place more weight on the tail. This causes the nose to lift and creates additional drag, also making it harder to paddle.

Riley is comfortable sitting right in front of me on the center of the board, and this is where I ask him to stay on long paddles. When we are just cruising along, he likes to ride up on the nose and look ahead. When Riley rides on the nose I take a step backward to help balance the board with his additional weight on the front. This helps keep the nose up out of the water.

Some dogs like Riley seem to smile when they are having a good time. Improve the chances of your dog having positive experiences by being prepared for situations you might not have expected.

Keep training fun and upbeat. When your dog stops smiling or shows signs of stress, end the session and go play.

Troubleshooting

Balance issues – If your dog demonstrates a pattern of jumping onto the board then jumping right off, remember that your dog's balance is being challenged. Just like us, dogs develop muscle memory, and they all develop it at different rates. Some dogs naturally have more balance than others. Building muscle memory could take several days, so it's important to stay positive and keep rewarding your dog for even the slightest bit of progress. If your dog didn't stay on the board very long and had a particularly challenging day, end training and do something fun with him. A game of fetch or a swim will help take the pressure off. Most dogs by nature want to please their owners and succeed at what they are being asked to do. Like us, they can become discouraged if they feel they keep failing. Don't let your dog end the day thinking he's disappointed you.

 TIP – If your dog is less confident than most and having trouble balancing, consider using a wobble board or buja board. These boards can easily be made or purchased. "They are great confidence builders as well as a great fitness tools. They teach balance and coordination while building core strength. PERFECT for the goals of SUPing with your PUP."
— *Teresa Mathern, K-9 master instructor*

Your dog moves around too much on the board – This is a common issue, especially for younger dogs that have a lots of energy or dogs that are nervous on the board. Have a designated area on the board that your dog knows is his space, and implement that into your training. A good way to start is by placing a towel, rubber mat, or deck padding on the floor and asking your dog to sit and stay on it. Once your dog understands that the towel is for staying, move the towel to the board. This will help your dog transfer these skills to the board. If you suspect your dog is the type that's going to dance all over the board, you may want to start with a towel on the floor before your first week of training. When you ask your dog to "hop on" the board, guide your dog to his space and ask your dog to stay. Always reward your dog for going to his space, and make sure he feels safe there. Give lots of praise and reinforcement.

If you find yourself out on the water and your dog starts pacing on the board, it may mean that he is nervous. Going from land to the water might have been a big jump for your dog, or the motion of the board could be stressful. Take a few steps back and work with your dog more in shallow water. Spend a week just pushing your dog around in shallow water with lots of praise and reward.

Kona has lots of puppy energy and likes to pace on the board. Part of her training included the use of a towel that marked her area to stay.

What to do when you and your dog fall off

It's going to happen—at some point you and your dog are going to knock each other into the water. It's a good idea to think about how you are going to handle this before it happens. As long as your dog is wearing his PFD and he's in your sight, I recommend you swim to your board first. If you are wearing a board leash, this is easier since you can just pull your board in. Get back on your board and retrieve your paddle, then paddle over to your dog. It's much easier to get your dog back on the board if you are already on it. Most dogs will swim back to the board or to shore on their own unless they become scared. If your dog

Slap the blade of your paddle in the water to brace yourself.

swims back to the board, he probably will try to claw his way back up with his front legs. When your dog starts reaching over the board, kneel down and grab the handle on his PFD with one hand and his bottom with the other to help him up and over. Don't stress or make a big deal over the fall. Stay calm; you don't want your dog to become upset. Falling off is part of learning, so expect it to happen and be prepared.

If at any point you anticipate that your dog is going to jump off, brace yourself by quickly crouching or kneeling. It's much easier to keep your balance if your center of gravity is low. You can also brace yourself by slapping the blade of your paddle into the water. When Riley and I get close to shore after a long paddle, he can't wait to hop off. Sometimes he'll jump before I give the command, so I've made it a habit to always kneel when we get close to land.

 TIP – "Be prepared for falls by practicing them. Pick a warm day in flat water and practice falling off your board and getting back on. Helping a big dog back on board can be tricky—so know what to expect!" *– Shawn Young, SUP instructor*

Surfing

Many people have asked us about surfing waves on our stand up paddleboard. This type of paddling is becoming increasingly popular and presents a different set of challenges for you and your dog.

When surfing waves, you will need to move up and down the length of your board to stay on the wave. Make sure that your dog either moves with you or can stay comfortable around the middle or nose of the board so you can adjust your position as you ride the wave.

Bryan Suratt, above, teaches his dog Happy to stand up paddle surf. "This was one of our first waves together, and you can tell she's uneasy by the way she's holding her ears," said the man locals on the North Shore of Oahu, Hawaii, call "Uncle Bryan."

Don't attempt surfing with your dog until you have both mastered flatwater paddling. If you are new to surfing, wait until you are very experienced in surf before taking your dog out. Start surfing in small waves so you can both get the feel for the board being pushed by the waves, and gradually work up to bigger waves. Paddleboard instructor Bryan Suratt, pictured above, explains training for surfing. *"I've been teaching surf lessons my entire adult life. It's what I do,"* he wrote. *"In teaching my dogs to stand up paddle surf, I've found there are a lot of things that are similar to teaching people. For some, the ocean is an unfamiliar environment. They're going to be a little nervous. ... Focus on the basics: Take it slow, keep them safe, meet them where they are, and go at their own pace. Give them lots of praise when they succeed and build them up, and eventually they will be just as hooked as you."*

Items to have in your first aid kit

It's not easy to carry everything you'd need for every type of medical situation you and your dog might find yourselves in. Having a few supplies on board for longer paddles can make a big difference until you can get back to land and help. Below is a basic list of items to carry on board for first aid situations. For a more complete list, pick up a copy of Randy Acker's book, *Field Guide: Dog First Aid Emergency Care for the Hunting, Working, and Outdoor Dog,* and carry it with you. It's a great reference guide for dog first aid.

Scissors
Tweezers
Sterile gauze pads
Adhesive tape
Vet tape, or tape that sticks to itself and not fur
Anti-bacterial pads
Antibiotic ointment (Neosporin)
Benadryl
Instant cold compress
3% hydrogen peroxide

Carry a small card in your kit with phone numbers for your vet, emergency clinic, and poison control. Include your personal and emergency contact information in case you are incapacitated. Also include your pet's microchip number, if he has one, and a photo of your dog in case you become separated.

Download a first aid and CPR manual, and keep it in your kit. Review the procedures before heading out on a long paddle. The American Red Cross offers courses in pet first aid, which covers managing breathing, treating wounds, and administering medicine. You may also want to check with your veterinarian for local classes and tips on how to handle emergency situations.

 TIP – Trim your dog's nails and any extra hair in between the pads of his feet before paddling. This will help reduce scratches on the board and keep your dog from slipping.

ACA | Canoe-Kayak-SUP-Raft-Rescue
sup-aca.org

American Kennel Club
akc.org

American Red Cross
redcross.org

Black Dog Paddle
blackdogpaddle.com

Colonial K9
colonialk9.com

Field Guide: Dog First Aid Emergency Care for the Hunting, Working, and Outdoor Dog
by Randy Acker, DVM

Ruffwear
ruffwear.com

Sunset Suratt Surf Academy
surfnorthshore.com

U.S. Coast Guard
uscg.mil

World Paddle Association
worldpaddleassociation.com

©Ruffwear & Ben Moon Foto

photo by Black Dog Paddle

photo by Black Dog Paddle

"We enjoy paddling with our dog so much, we made her our corporate logo."
— *Bryan Smith, owner of Black Dog Paddle*

Acknowledgements

I'd like to thank my husband, **John Schultz**. Many years ago he opened my eyes to the wonders of nature, and without his constant love and support this book would not have been possible. His trust and encouragement allows me the freedom to explore the world. I am so lucky to have him in my life as my partner and soul mate.

Special thanks to **Shawn Young**, a good friend and paddleboard instructor who helped me develop my skills as a stand up paddler. Shawn encouraged me and Riley to sit in on his lessons and paddle with new people in our community. He is also responsible for many of the pictures in this book. Thanks, Shawn, for helping us share our story with the world.

Thanks to **Ruffwear** for outfitting Riley in the safest dog gear ever made. From Riley's leash to his PFD, Ruffwear helps keep my best friend safe and comfortable on our adventures.

To **Dr. Helen Jewett** and the staff at **Hartwood Animal Hospital**, thank you for always looking out for Riley's health and well being. I am forever grateful for the compassion you have shown Riley and Kona.

Lisa Chinn Marvashti, Neva Trenis, and **Laura Moyer,** this book would not have been possible without your skills in wordsmithing and editing. Thank you for helping me craft my ideas and words into something I can be proud of.

Teresa Mathern at **Colonial K9,** thank you for your suggestions to this training plan. Over the years I have learned so much from working with you and all the wonderful trainers at Colonial K9. Thank you all for giving me the skills to apply what you have taught us to paddling.

 Chris Stec and the **ACA**, thank you for your invaluable thoughts on safety. This book is so much better because of it. And thank you for providing me with the skills to become an instructor so that I can continue to share this wonderful sport with others.

Thank you to everyone else who encouraged us and supported this project.

Finally, thank you **Mom**—you never let me forget that I needed to write a book.

19539649R00023

Made in the USA
San Bernardino, CA
02 March 2015